BENJAMIN BRITTEN

Selections from *The Beggar's Opera*
Realized from the original airs of John Gay's Ballad Opera (1728)

16 Selections
13 Solos and 3 Duets
for various voice types

Words by John Gay

Edited by Richard Walters

Vocal Score by Arthur Oldham

Also available: Vocal Score (HL48009753; ISMN 979-0-060-03073-4), Study Score (HL48011566; ISMN 979-0-060-09687-7)

BOOSEY & HAWKES

DISTRIBUTED BY

7777 W. BLUEMOUND RD. P.O. BOX 13819 MILWAUKEE, WI 53213

www.boosey.com
www.halleonard.com

CHARACTERS OF THE OPERA

Beggar .... Speaking role
Mrs. Peachum .... Mezzo-soprano
Mr. Peachum .... Bass
Polly .... Mezzo-soprano
Captain Macheath .... Tenor
Filch .... Tenor (or speaking role)
Lockit .... Baritone
Lucy Lockit .... Soprano
Mrs. Trapes .... Contralto
Mrs. Vixen ....
Suky Tawdry ....
Mrs. Coaxer... Ladies of the Town
Dolly Trull... (divided into
Mrs. Slammekin... Sopranos, Mezzo-sopranos
Molly Brazen .... and Contraltos)
Jenny Diver ....
Betty Doxy ....
Harry Paddington ....
Ben Budge.. Gentlemen of the Road
Wat Dreary .... (divided equally into
Mat of the Mint .... Tenors, Baritones
Jemmy Twitcher... and Basses)
Nimming Ned..

FIRST PERFORMANCE CAST

This version of **The Beggar's Opera** was first staged by the English Opera Group
at the Arts Theatre, Cambridge, England, on May 24, 1948.

CAST

Beggar... Gladys Parr
Mrs. Peachum .... Flora Nielsen
Mr. Peachum .... George James
Polly .... Nancy Evans
Captain Macheath .... Peter Pears
Filch .... Norman Platt
Lockit .... Otakar Kraus
Lucy Lockit .... Rose Hill
Mrs. Trapes .... Gladys Parr
Mrs. Vixen... Lesley Duff
Suky Tawdry .... Lily Kettlewell
Mrs. Coaxer... Catherine Lawson
Dolly Trull.. Gladys Parr
Mrs. Slammekin... Elisabeth Parry
Molly Brazen .... Anne Sharp
Jenny Diver .... Jennifer Vyvyan
Betty Doxy .... Mildred Watson
Harry Paddington .... Roy Ashton
Ben Budge.. Denis Dowling
Wat Dreary .... John Highcock
Mat of the Mint .... Norman Lumsden
Jemmy Twitcher... Norman Platt
Nimming Ned.. Max Worthley

Conductor: Benjamin Britten
Producer: Tyrone Guthrie
Assistant Producer: Basil Coleman
Scenery and Costumes: Tanya Moiseiwitsch

CONTENTS

PREFATORY NOTE FROM THE STUDY SCORE

The years 1946-48 were characterized by Britten's phenomenal creativity. With *Peter Grimes* only just behind him (1945), he launched out in 1946 with *The Rape of Lucretia*; and in 1947 he followed up his new concept of chamber opera—though the idea had been with him even before *Grimes* was composed—with *Albert Herring* (the playing time of which equals that of *Grimes*) and, in 1948, with **The Beggar's Opera**. Three operas at the rate of one a year—the cumulative total of their duration represents some 5 hours 49 minutes of continuous music according to the composer's own timings!—is prodigality indeed. As if that were not enough, the very act of creating these chamber operas as a response to the need for a musical theatre that was something other than 'grand' opera (with all the implications that term has for complementary resources) itself created a need for a newly constituted opera company to produce and perform the works as they came off Britten's production line. The initial collaboration with Glyndebourne on *Lucretia* had not worked out. Hence, in 1947, the establishing of the English Opera Group, which landed Britten with a fresh set of responsibilities. He was not only the company's chief composer but also had to busy himself with policy, administration, strenuous touring and a lot of coaching and conducting of his own works.

There is no doubt that a pre-existing text and source of melodies must have been a godsend to Britten in the circumstances in which he found himself in 1947 and 1948. But it would be a mistake to conclude that it was principally as a solution to meeting impossible deadlines that Britten took on *The Beggar's Opera* with enthusiasm. It was rather, I suggest, because the undertaking gave him the opportunity to exercise on a major scale and in the most elaborate form a part of his creativity that was fundamental to his compositional character, his interests and his techniques. In short, Britten did not so much "arrange" his tunes as treat them as if he had composed them himself. He strips them—quite ruthlessly, one might think—of their independent histories and substitutes his own. Indeed, the only history we need to know in the context of this 1948 version of *The Beggar's Opera* is the composer's, i.e. Britten's. The historicizing approach—even his own—"each generation sees [the tunes] from a different aspect"— is quite beside the point. If the work survives, as I believe it will, it will survive as, and because of, what it is: a highly original and entirely typical addition to the Britten operatic canon.

To comprehend what Britten was up to, then, we need examine nothing else but the evolution of his own music, and in particular his relationship to folksong. A central text here is what he wrote in his diary on March 3, 1933, when he was a student at the Royal College of Music in London. He had just heard on the radio "two brilliant folk-song arrangements of Percy Grainger—17 Come Sunday & Father & Son, knocking all the V. Williams and R.O. Morris arrangements into a cocked-hat".

Grainger was among the boldest of twentieth-century setters of folksong. There was no seeking after a bogus "authenticity" (and this despite the fact that Grainger was a serious collector of folksongs); his arrangements, though sometimes exquisitely lyrical, were not predominantly "pastoral" (as, say, were Vaughan Williams's); he pioneered the concept of *orchestral* settings, of high imagination and vivid color; he developed with great skill the ballad-like or quasi-dramatic narrative folksong, and extended form, in which an elaborate accompaniment was tailor-made to respond to the unfolding sequence of events; and each setting, one might claim, was stamped by his inimitable personality.

These were all initiatives and options that Britten was himself to explore. He was to bring a similar graphic inventiveness to the narrative folksong, e.g. "Sweet Polly Oliver" or "The Ash Grove". It was an approach that was lyrical when appropriate but rarely pastoral; abstained from any attempt at evoking "authenticity"; and, like Grainger's, took up the challenge of the orchestral setting. This last dimension has a particular bearing on *The Beggar's Opera*, in which, just as in the orchestral versions of his folksong settings, Britten reveals an extraordinary instrumental imagination. Each number in the opera wears an individual orchestral dress that perfectly matches tune, text and the dramatic or lyric moment. There is no uniform orchestra or orchestration; each number has its *own* orchestra. This is a dazzling display of chamber orchestral virtuosity, perhaps unequalled among Britten's works for the same medium; but there was an earlier precedent, *Paul Bunyan*, the operetta (1941) on which Britten had collaborated with W.H. Auden, each number of which unfolds a fresh, independent orchestra extrapolated from the existing instrumental resources. (It seems highly probable, though still incredible, that Britten composed his realization of *The Beggar's Opera* directly into full score; no sketches whatsoever survive to suggest otherwise.)

But if Britten's bold orchestral approach to folksong was in the spirit of Grainger's, there was one dimension at least in which Britten's settings were markedly distinct. Grainger's personality had often manifested itself in the characteristic richness of the Graingeresque harmony with which his arrangements are saturated. Less so Britten's, where it is *counterpoint* that was at the top of his agenda, as his reference to "canonizing" in a letter to Peter Pears of March 17, 1948 makes clear. In one number after another, not excluding the Overture, it is forcibly brought home that counterpoint, and canon in particular, is fundamental to the compositional process that characterizes the opera. (This unique feature of the score runs like a continuous thread throughout the sequence of numbers.)

The incessant "canonizing", to use Britten's own description, yet further reflects what had always been one of the composer's preoccupations from his early years onwards: how much in fact was to be got out of the *single line*, whether it be the fugue subject of the finale of the *Bridge Variations* (1937), a folksong, or numbers like "Cease your funning" (No. 34) or "Why how now, Madam flirt!" (No. 35), from *The Beggar's Opera*. It was an abiding preoccupation that makes his concentration on the potentialities of the single line that distinguishes the heterophonic textures of the later church parables (1964-68) seem an entirely logical and inevitable evolution.

All this indicates that *The Beggar's Opera* is not a "sport" among Britten's operas but an integral part of the totality of theatrical works, from *Paul Bunyan* to *Death in Venice*, that was his prodigiously rich legacy. As for the plot, are we surprised that Britten's imagination was excited by it? After all Macheath is yet another of Britten's doomed heroes, tormented by love, the victim of treachery, and only saved in the nick of time by the conventions of "opera" coming to his rescue.

It was a release that Britten permitted none other of his tragic heroes to enjoy.

Donald Mitchell

PLOT SYNOPSIS

Act I

The Beggar introduces his opera, calling for the overture. The actors are seen setting the stage during the overture. The story begins with a thief-catcher, Mr. Peachum, going over his accounts. He and his assistant, Filch, discuss the criminals they employ. Mrs. Peachum joins the conversation, expressing her concern for her daughter Polly and her relationship with the nefarious highwayman, Macheath. Having hung their hopes for betterment on Polly marrying well, the Peachums are angry to learn that Polly has secretly married Macheath. The Peachums plot to do away with Macheath and live well on Polly's inheritance. But Polly warns her husband and sends him away for safety. Macheath flees to a tavern where his cohorts are singing and drinking. He tells them to spread the word that he has quit their band of thieves, promising to continue meeting them in secret. Macheath sings a song to women in general and then sends for some women to entertain him. He is surprised and furious when the women signal for Mr. Peachum and the Constables, who arrest him.

Act II

Macheath bribes Lockit, the jailor, for the lightest fetters available, blaming his fate on women. Macheath had once proposed marriage to Lucy, the jailor's daughter. She arrives, berating Macheath for promising marriage and then abandoning her for Polly. He convinces her that he is not really married to Polly. Lucy pleads her beloved's case to her father, but Lockit has agreed with Peachum that the two will split Macheath's fortune after he is hanged. Macheath presses Lucy to bribe her father, but Polly arrives calling for her husband. Macheath tries to spurn Polly and pacify Lucy. Arguing, the two women are taken away by their fathers. Lucy returns to the jail later to set Macheath free.

Act III

When pressed, Lucy admits to her father that she freed Macheath. Peachum and Lockit enter an uneasy alliance to recapture Macheath, with the help of Mrs. Trapes. Lucy tries, unsuccessfully, to poison Polly. Both women are overcome with grief to hear of Macheath's recapture. He is bound for the gallows. Lucy and Polly say their sad goodbyes to him and Macheath slips into despair. At the last moment Ben Budge calls for a reprieve. Mat of the Mint tells the audience to join the cry for reprieve. A reprieve is granted, despite the Beggar's objections, and the opera ends with a joyous dance.

NOTES ON THE SONGS

'Tis woman that seduces all mankind (Filch)
Act 1, No. 2, Scene: Peachum's lock

Peachum and his assistant, Filch, discuss the situations of the hoodlums in their employ. They agree that women are invaluable to men in their trade. Filch sings about the seductive, deceitful nature of women. A note in the vocal and study scores states that this song can either be sung by Filch alone or divided among the "Ladies of the Town."

If love the virgin's heart invade (Mrs. Peachum)
Act 1, No. 4, Scene: Peachum's lock

The Peachums worry that Polly might marry Macheath. Mrs. Peachum sings of her fear that Polly might lose her innocence if she's not married soon.

Virgins arc like the fair flower (Polly)
Act 1, No. 6, Scene: Peachum's lock

Mrs. Peachum leads Filch off for a drink, hoping that he will divulge information about Polly and Macheath. Polly and Mr. Peachum enter, Polly singing this reassurance that she understands the value and allure of virginity and can take care of herself.

I, like a ship in storms, was tossed (Polly)
Act 1, No. 10, Scene: Peachum's lock

The facts of Polly's marriage have come out. Angry at first, her parents calm down and apparently resign themselves to the news. Polly sings this song of relief and joy.

A fox may steal your hens, Sir (Mr. and Mrs. Peachum)
Act 1, No. 11, Scene: Peachum's lock

The Peachums plan Macheath's impeachment and hanging. They worry that the rogue may have more than one wife, which would jeopardize Polly's legal right to inherit his fortune. In this duet the Peachums agree that of all the thieves in this world, lawyers are the worst.

The miser thus a shilling sees (Macheath and Polly)
Act 1, No. 18, Scene: Peachum's lock

Having warned Macheath of her parents' scheme to have him hanged, Polly sends Macheath away for his safety. They part, gazing back at one another fondly and singing this song of various farewells.

If the heart of a man is depressed with cares (Macheath)
Act 1, No. 21, Scene: A tavern near Newgate

As Macheath's cohorts depart for a night of crime, he ponders his love for women. He sings of their charms, ending by crying, "I must have women."

Man may escape from rope and gun (Macheath)
Act 2, No. 26, Scene: Newgate Prison

Macheath has been arrested. No stranger to prison life, he bribes Lockit for the lightest fetters available. Despondent, he sings from his cell, blaming his woeful ruin on women.

Thus when a good housewife sees a rat/How cruel are the traytors (Lucy)

Act 2, No. 27 and 28, Scene: Newgate Prison

Lucy Lockit, to whom Macheath has made a promise of marriage, arrives at the prison. She rails in anger, having heard of his marriage to Polly, and sings about a housewife's delight in throwing the rat to the cat. When Macheath calls himself her husband "in every respect but the form," the insulted Lucy sings about the cruelty of men.

Why how now, Madam Flirt! (Lucy and Polly)

Act 2, No. 35, Scene: Another part of the prison

Macheath, denying his marriage to Polly, seems to be winning back Lucy's affections. Polly arrives, calling for her husband, but Macheath denies his marriage to her. Polly accuses Lucy of behaving inappropriately toward a woman and her husband, and Lucy threatens to have Polly thrown out of the jail. The two women burst into this musical catfight.

When young at the bar/Ungrateful Macheath! (Lucy)

Act 3, No. 37 and 38, Scene: Newgate

Lockit accuses Lucy of freeing Macheath. She blames Polly and Mr. Peachum. Unconvinced, Lockit scolds her and says that her education should have made her savvier. Lucy responds, singing about how her father taught her to use kisses as trickery. She confesses to freeing Macheath, adding that she now believes that Polly is his wife. Lucy tells her father that she could murder Polly, expressing her fury in "Ungrateful Macheath!"

Thus gamesters united in friendship (Lockit)

Act 3, No. 39, Scene: Newgate

Aware that Peachum has a plot, Lockit resolves to trick the details out of him and turn the affair to his own advantage. Lockit's song states that there is no honor among thieves.

I'm like a skiff on the ocean tossed (Lucy)

Act 3, No. 43b, Scene: Newgate

Mr. Peachum, Lockit and Mrs. Trapes plot Macheath's recapture. Knowing that Macheath has returned to Polly, Lucy is torn apart by jealousy, rage, love and fear. She begins singing about being tossed like a skiff on the ocean, eventually resolving to have her revenge.

O cruel, cruel case! (Macheath)

Act 3, No. 53, Scene: The condemned hold

A melancholy Macheath awaits his own hanging. Hopeless, he expresses his woe, asserting that only strong drink can raise his spirits. He sings on, bemoaning his fate, wailing that if the rich were held to the same punishment as the poor, multitudes would swing from the tree.

INSTRUMENTATION

Flute (doubling Piccolo), Oboe (doubling Cor Anglais), Clarinet in B♭ and A,

Bassoon, Horn in F, *Timpani and Percussion (1), Harp, String Quartet, Double Bass.

* triangle, block, tambourine, side drum, tenor drum, bass drum, suspended cymbal, gong

'Tis woman that seduces all mankind

Words by JOHN GAY

JOHN GAY
realized by BENJAMIN BRITTEN

*There is a note in the vocal score which states that this song may either be sung by Filch alone or divided among the Ladies of the Town.

with __ our __ Hearts. 'Tis Wom-an that se - duc - es __

all __ Man - kind, By Her we first were taught the __ wheed - ling __ Arts: Her

ver - y eyes can cheat; When most __ she's __ kind, She tricks __ us __ of our Mon-ey

with _ our _ Hearts.

For her, like wolves by night We

cresc.

roam _ for _ Prey, And prac-tise ev -'ry fraud to bribe _ her _ Charms; For

mf

dim.

Suits of Love, like Law, are won _ by _ Pay, and Beau - ty _ must be fee'd in -

to _ our _ arms. _____

ppp

If love the virgin's heart invade

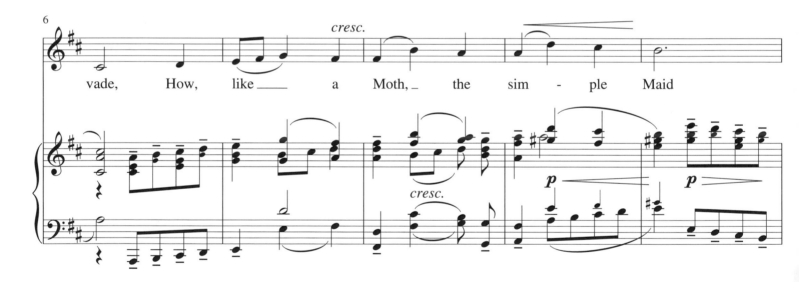

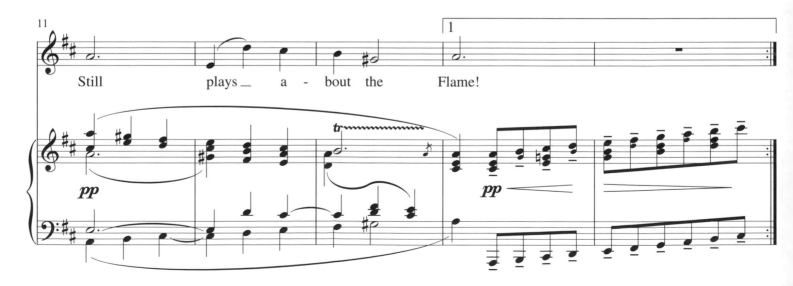

Virgins are like the fair flower

plucked, 'tis no long- er al- lur - ing; To Co- vent Gar- den 'tis__ sent__ (as yet

sweet); There fades, and shrinks, and grows past all__ en - dur - ing.

Rots,__ stinks, and__ dies,__ and is__ trod__ un - der feet!__

I, like a ship in storms, was tossed

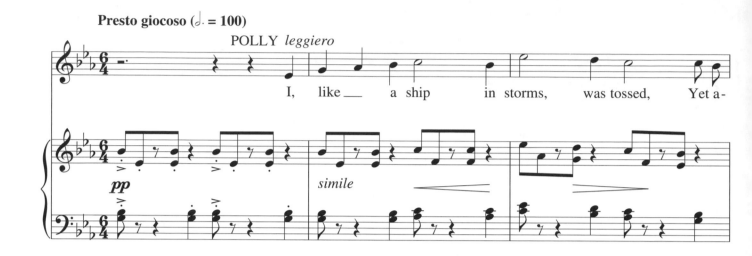

waves are laid,___ my du - ty's paid; O joy be-yond ex-

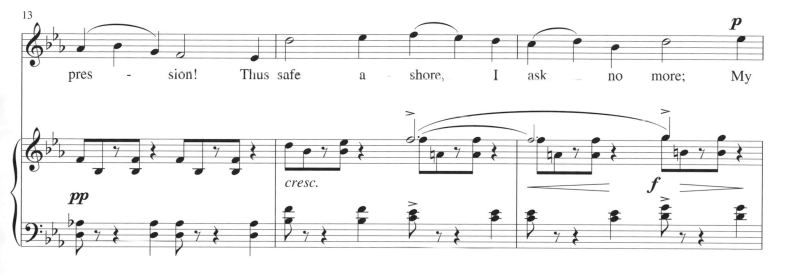

pres - sion! Thus safe a - shore, I ask no more; My

all is in my pos - ses - sion, pos - ses - sion, My all is in my pos -

ses - sion!___

A fox may steal your hens, Sir

(Duet)

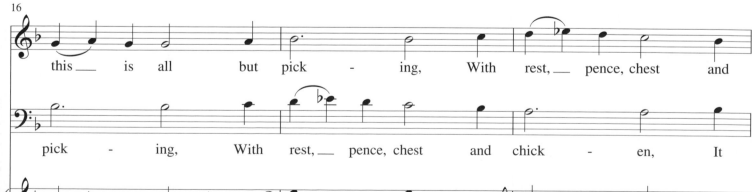

Man may escape from rope and gun

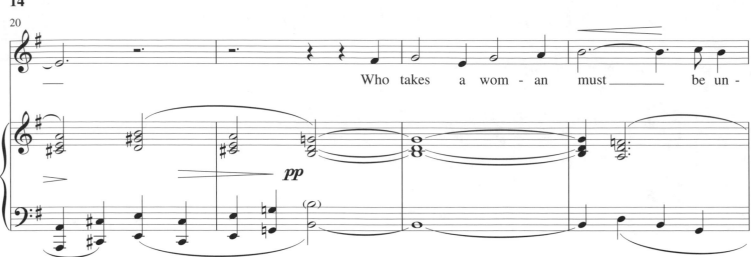

Who takes a wom - an must _____ be un -

done, That bas - i - lisk is sure _____ to __

kill. The _ fly _____ that sips

trea - cle is lost in the sweets; So he that tastes

wom - an, wom - an, wom - an, he _____ that tastes wom - an, ru - in _ meets.

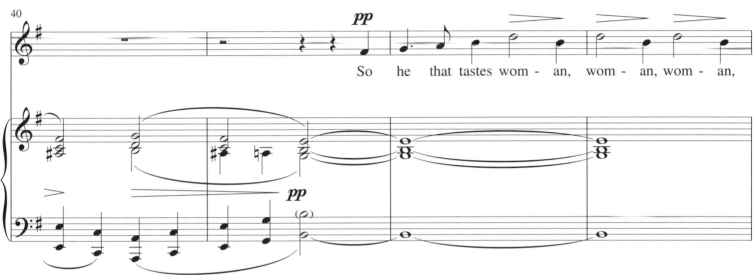

So he that tastes wom - an, wom - an, wom - an,

wom - an, He that tastes wom - an ru - in _ meets.

The miser thus a shilling sees
(Duet)

Andante lento (♩ = 54)

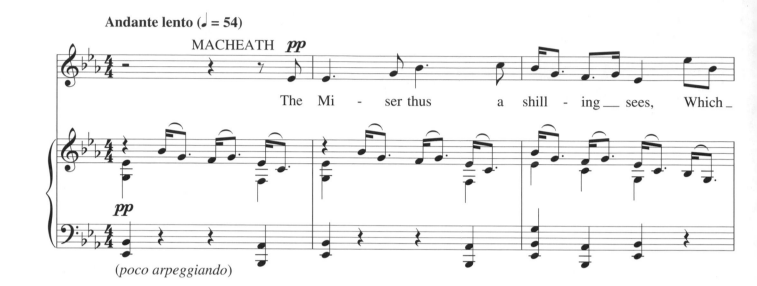

MACHEATH *pp*

The Mi - ser thus a shill - ing sees, Which

pp

(poco arpeggiando)

he's o - bliged to pay, With sighs re - signs it

p

by de - grees, And fears 'tis gone for

p

dim.

pp

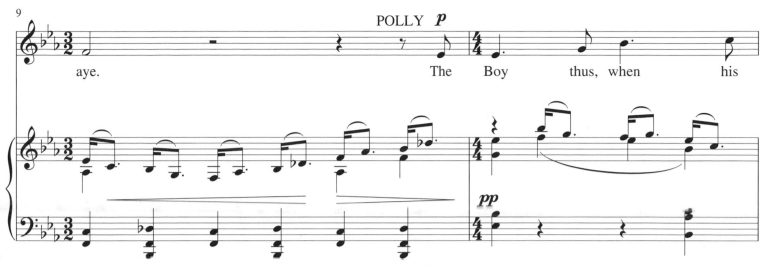

POLLY

aye. The Boy thus, when his

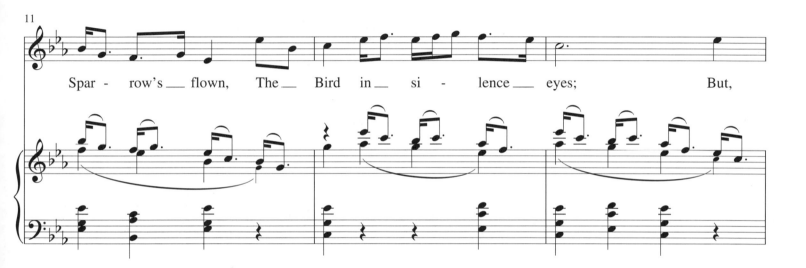

Spar - row's __ flown, The __ Bird in __ si - lence __ eyes; But,

soon __ as __ out of __ sight 'tis __ gone, Whines, __

If the heart of a man is depressed with cares

Ro - ses and Lil - ies her cheeks dis - close, But her ripe lips are more

sweet than those. Press her, Ca - ress her, With bliss - es, Her kiss - es Dis -

solve us in pleas-ure, and soft re-pose. soft re-pose.

Thus when a good housewife sees a rat/
How cruel are the traytors

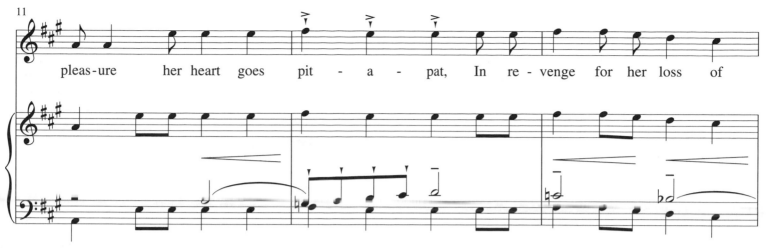

pleas-ure her heart goes pit - a - pat, In re-venge for her loss of

ba - - con, Then she throws him To the dog or cat, to be

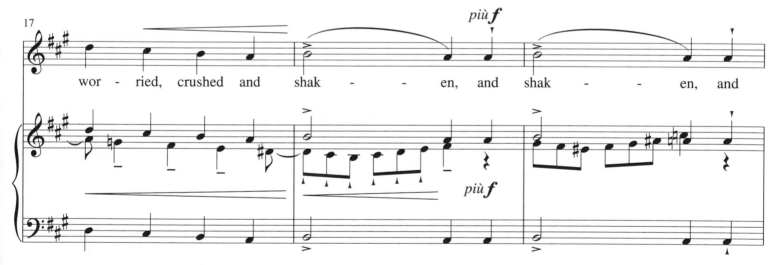

più f

wor-ried, crushed and shak - - en, and shak - - en, and

ff

shak - - - - - - en!

ev - er steals_ a shil-ling, Through shame_ the guilt_ con-ceals; ___ In

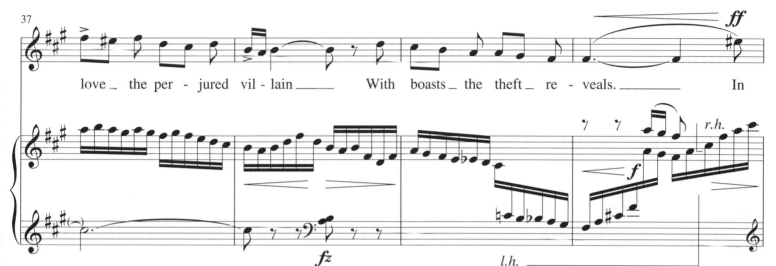

love_ the per-jured vil-lain ___ With boasts_ the theft_ re-veals. ___ In

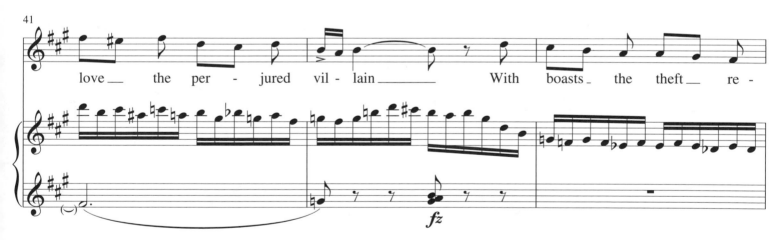

love_ the per-jured vil-lain ___ With boasts_ the theft_ re-

veals. ___

Why how now, Madam Flirt!

(Duet)

When young at the bar/Ungrateful Macheath!

taught me to ___ score, And ___ bid me be free of my

lips, and ___ no more. I was

kissed by the Par - son, the Squire, and the Sot; When the guest was de -

part - ed, ___ the ___ kiss ___ was ___ for - got. But ___

his kiss was so sweet and so close-ly he pressed, That I

lan - guished and pined till I grant - ed the rest.

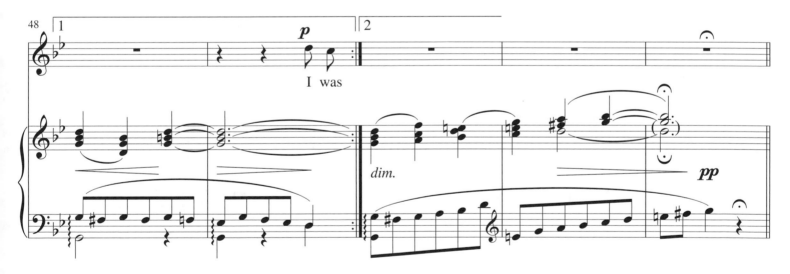

I was

Presto (♩. = 126)

Un - grate - ful Mac -

I'm like a skiff on the ocean tossed

an - chor lost, De -sert -ed and all for -lorn._____ I'm

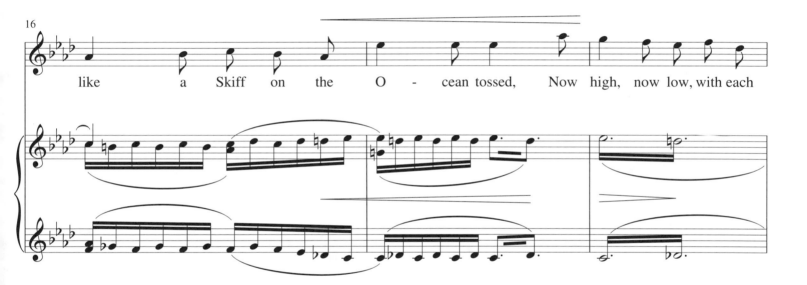

like a Skiff on the O - cean tossed, Now high, now low, with each

bil - low borne, With her rud - der broke, and her an - chor lost, De -

sert - ed and all for - lorn._____ While thus I lie rol - ling and

tos - sing all night, That Pol - ly lies sport - ing on seas of de - light! Re -

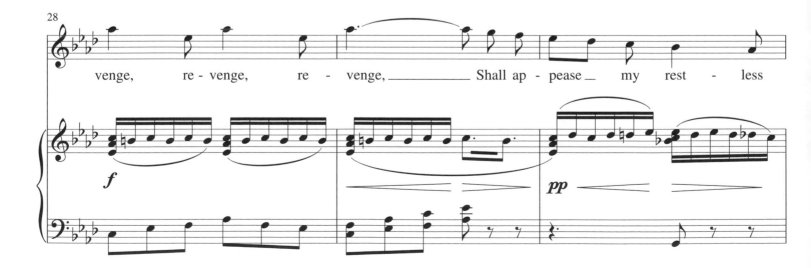

venge, re - venge, re - venge,_____ Shall ap - pease_ my rest - less

sprite! _____ Re - venge, re - venge, re - venge, re - venge, re -

venge, _____ shall ap - pease my rest - less

sprite!

O cruel, cruel case!

Scene: The Condemned Hold

MACHEATH, in a melancholy posture.

O cru - el, cru - el ___ case! Must I suf - fer this ___ dis -

grace?

Allegretto (♩ slower than before)

Of __ all the friends in __ time of grief, When __ threat - 'ning Death _____ looks grim - mer, __ Not __ one so sure can __ bring re - lief, As __ this best friend, _____ a brim - mer.

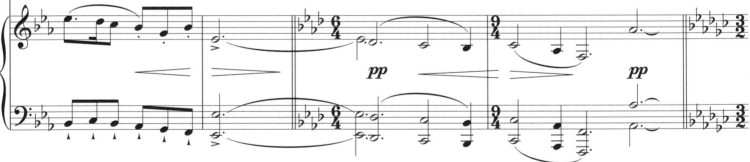

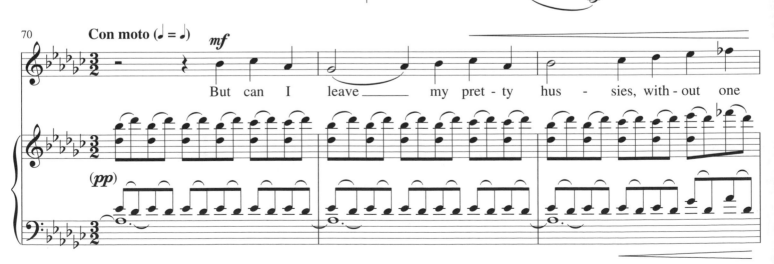

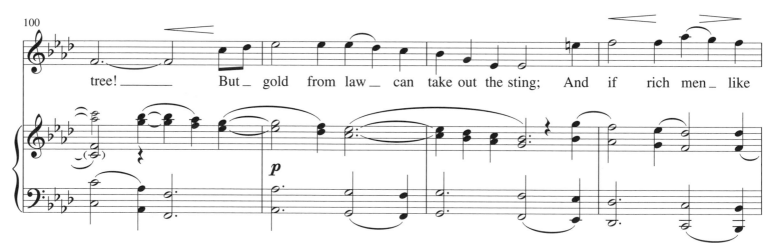

Tyburn Tree: the place of public execution for Middlesex until 1783: the gallows.

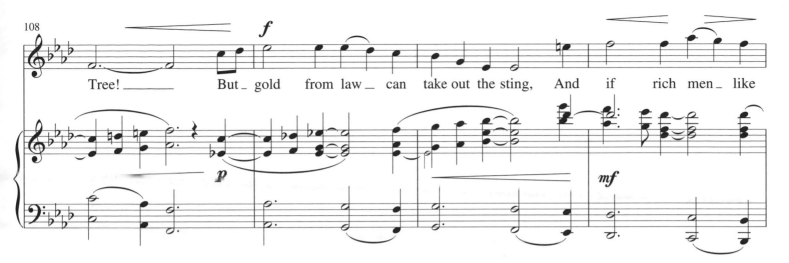

Tree! _____ But _ gold from law _ can take out the sting, And if rich men _ like

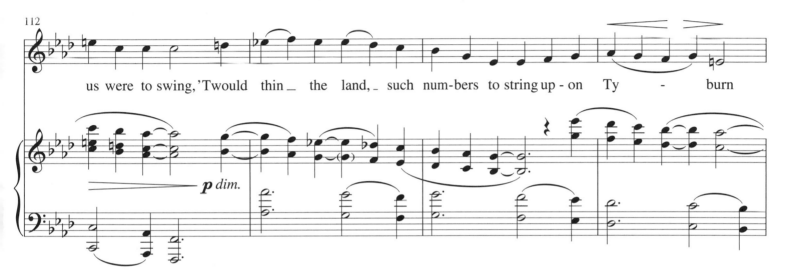

us were to swing, 'Twould thin _ the land, _ such num-bers to string up - on Ty - burn

Tree. _____

Thus gamesters united in friendship

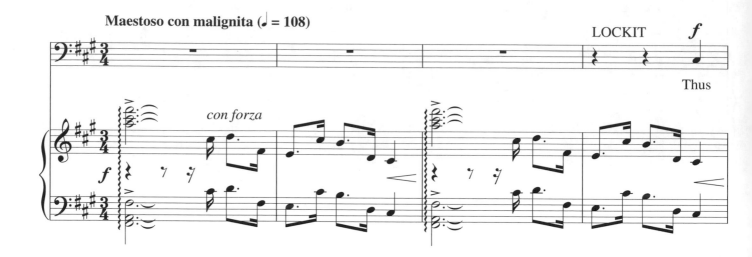

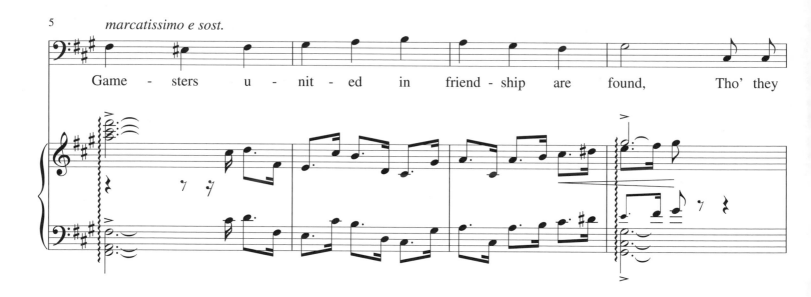

They flock to their prey at the dice box-'s sound, And join to pro-mote one an-o-ther's de-ceit. But if by mis-hap, They fail of a chap, To keep in their hands, they each

29
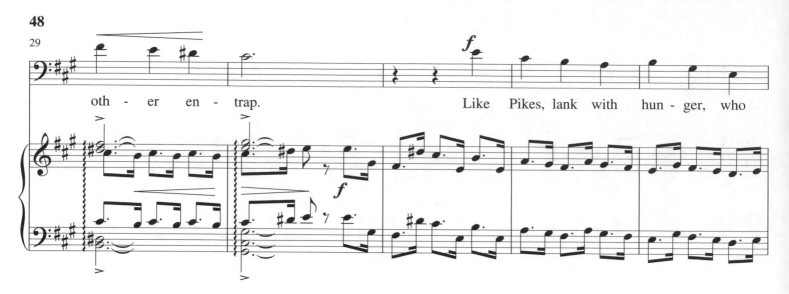

oth - er en - trap. Like Pikes, lank with hun - ger, who

34

miss of their ends, They bite their com - pan - ions, and

39

prey on their friends. But

44